CHAMPIONS
IN THE MAKING

Preface

Welcome to "Inspirational Sports Stories for Young Readers: Champions in the Making." As the pages unfold before you, you are about to embark on a journey into the world of triumph, teamwork, and tenacity—where young athletes discover the true essence of becoming champions.

In these tales, we've woven narratives that resonate with the spirit of every young reader, encouraging them to dream big and find inspiration in the pursuit of their sporting passions. From the soccer fields to the basketball courts, the skate parks to the sailing waves, our characters represent the diverse and dynamic nature of sports.

As you delve into the victories and challenges faced by these young athletes, you'll witness the transformative power of sportsmanship, perseverance, and the unwavering belief in oneself. These stories are more than just accounts of athletic achievements; they are reflections of the indomitable spirit that resides within every child who aspires to be a champion.

May these pages inspire the young minds turning them to understand that, no matter the obstacles, every setback is a setup for a greater comeback. Whether you are a budding athlete, an aspiring artist, or a reader seeking tales of empowerment, "Champions in the Making" is a celebration of the human spirit and the resilience that defines us all.

So, join us in the world of sports and dreams, where every victory is a collective triumph, and every setback is an opportunity for growth. The journey begins now.

Warm regards,

Table of Content

1. Soaring Soccer Stars: Emily and Jake's Winning Game

Once upon a sunny afternoon in the vibrant town of Brooksville, Emily and Jake, two inseparable friends, found themselves on the soccer field, surrounded by cheers and the unmistakable hum of excitement. Their friendship, rooted in a shared passion for soccer, was about to be tested in the most thrilling way possible.

Emily, with her fiery red hair and a perpetual grin, was known for her lightning-fast footwork and strategic playmaking. Jake, a tall and energetic boy with a perpetual twinkle in his eye, was the team's defensive powerhouse. Together, they made an unstoppable duo on the field, earning them the nickname "The Dynamic Duo" among their teammates.

On this particular day, the Brooksville soccer team was gearing up for the championship match against their rivals, the Cobalt Comets. The stakes were high, and the entire town turned out to witness the clash of the titans.

The first half of the game was intense, with both teams displaying remarkable skill and determination. Emily and Jake coordinated seamlessly, with Emily scoring a brilliant goal, putting Brooksville in the lead. The crowd erupted in cheers as they witnessed the sheer brilliance of the Dynamic Duo.

However, soccer, like life, is unpredictable. In the second half, the Cobalt Comets launched a relentless offensive, catching the Brooksville team off guard. The score was now tied, and the pressure mounted.

As the final minutes ticked away, Emily and Jake rallied their teammates, instilling a renewed sense of determination. With seconds left on the clock, Jake executed a breathtaking defensive move, intercepting a powerful shot from the opposing team. The referee's whistle blew, signaling the end of regular time.

Overtime brought a surge of adrenaline, and both teams fought fiercely. It was Emily who emerged as the hero, scoring the winning goal with a spectacular bicycle kick. The Brooksville team and their supporters erupted in jubilation, celebrating a hard-fought victory.

In the midst of the cheers, Emily and Jake shared a triumphant glance, recognizing that their teamwork and friendship had prevailed. The championship trophy was hoisted high, and the Dynamic Duo's names were etched into Brooksville's soccer history.

As the sun set over the soccer field, Emily and Jake reveled in the joy of victory, knowing that their journey had only just begun. Little did they know that more adventures awaited, both on and off the field, as their friendship and love for the game continued to soar.

2. Leap of Courage: Chloe and Max in the Gymnastics Spotlight

In the quiet town of Harmony Grove, Chloe and Max, two inseparable friends, discovered a shared passion for gymnastics that would propel them into an extraordinary journey of courage, friendship, and self-discovery.

Chloe, a spirited and determined girl with a penchant for pushing boundaries, first set foot in the local gymnastics gym when she was just six years old. From the moment her tiny feet touched the mat, the thrill of somersaults and handstands captured her heart. Chloe's infectious enthusiasm soon caught the attention of her best friend, Max.

Max, a quiet and reserved boy, watched Chloe's daring flips and twists from the sidelines with a mix of awe and curiosity. One day, unable to resist the allure any longer, he joined Chloe in the gymnastics gym. Little did they know that this shared interest would not only change their lives but also create a bond that would withstand the test of time.

Their journey through the world of gymnastics was not without its challenges. Chloe faced the daunting uneven bars with determination, while Max grappled with the heights of the vaulting horse. Together, they supported each other through the falls, the bruises, and the moments of self-doubt.

As the years passed, Chloe and Max progressed through the ranks of local competitions, their skills and confidence growing with every routine. Yet, the true test awaited them at the prestigious Harmony Grove Gymnastics Championships. The pressure was palpable as the entire town gathered to witness their leap into the gymnastics spotlight.

The day of the championships arrived, and Chloe and Max faced a nerve-wracking mix of excitement and anxiety. The mats seemed bouncier, the balance beam narrower, and the cheers of the crowd louder than ever before. It was their moment to shine, and they were determined to give it their all.

Chloe's routine was a mesmerizing display of grace and power, her flips and tumbles executed flawlessly. The crowd erupted in applause, and Chloe's eyes gleamed with pride. Now, it was Max's turn. The vault awaited him like a towering challenge, but with Chloe's encouragement echoing in his ears, he summoned the courage to take the leap.

As Max soared through the air and landed with unwavering precision, the gym fell into a hushed awe. The judges, the audience, and even

Chloe herself were left breathless by Max's display of courage. Their combined efforts earned them not only the admiration of their community but also the coveted Harmony Grove Gymnastics Trophy.

Chloe and Max's leap of courage not only secured their places in the gymnastics spotlight but also taught the town of Harmony Grove a valuable lesson about determination, support, and the strength that comes from facing challenges head-on. From that day forward, Chloe and Max became local heroes, inspiring young gymnasts to take their own leaps of courage and reach for the stars.

And so, in the heart of Harmony Grove, Chloe and Max's gymnastics journey continued, filled with new challenges, lasting friendships, and the unwavering belief that the most remarkable feats are achieved when you take that leap of courage.

3. Basketball Buzz: Olivia and Alex's Slam Dunk Journey

Once upon a time in the small town of Groveville, where the sound of bouncing basketballs echoed through the neighborhood, two friends, Olivia and Alex, were about to embark on a basketball adventure that would change their lives.

Olivia, with her unruly curls and infectious laughter, had a passion for the game that matched the energy of the court itself. She could dribble, shoot, and pass with finesse that belied her young age. Her friend, Alex, was the tech whiz of the duo. Always carrying a tablet loaded with basketball stats and strategies, he had an uncanny ability to analyze the game from a different perspective.

One sunny afternoon, the two friends found a worn-out basketball in the corner of the park. It was a bit deflated, but to Olivia and Alex, it was a treasure waiting to be discovered. They decided to form their own two-person basketball team, and thus began their slam dunk journey.

At first, their attempts were comical. Olivia would leap with all her might, aiming for the hoop, while Alex provided play-by-play commentary and statistics in the background. Despite the missed shots and fumbled passes, they were having the time of their lives.

One day, as they practiced at their favorite court, they caught the attention of Coach Miller, the seasoned basketball coach from Groveville Elementary. Impressed by their enthusiasm, he offered to mentor them. Under Coach Miller's guidance, Olivia and Alex honed their skills, learning the importance of teamwork and strategy.

The local basketball tournament was just around the corner, and Olivia and Alex were determined to make a mark. With the support of their families and the guidance of Coach Miller, they trained tirelessly. Olivia's speed and agility paired perfectly with Alex's precision passes and three-point accuracy.

As the day of the tournament arrived, Olivia and Alex faced teams with more experience and height. But what they lacked in stature, they made up for in heart and determination. The crowd watched in awe as Olivia drove to the hoop with lightning speed, and Alex's three-pointers found the mark.

In the championship game, with seconds left on the clock, the score tied, Olivia dribbled past defenders, passing the ball to Alex. With a swift motion, he took the shot, and the ball sailed through the hoop, securing victory for their team.

The basketball court erupted in cheers as Olivia and Alex celebrated their Slam Dunk Journey triumph. From that day forward, their story inspired young athletes in Groveville, proving that with passion, teamwork, and a bit of basketball buzz, anyone could become a slam dunk champion.

And so, in the heart of Groveville, the legend of Olivia and Alex's Slam Dunk Journey lived on, a tale whispered in the bouncing echoes of basketballs for generations to come.

4. Skateboard Legends: Tyler and Ava's Wheels of Determination

Once upon a sunlit suburb, in a town buzzing with youthful energy, lived Tyler and Ava. These two friends shared a common passion that echoed through the concrete ramps and echoed in the rhythmic clatter of wheels on pavement: skateboarding.

Tyler, a lanky teenager with a shock of unruly hair, had always found solace in the smooth glide and daring tricks of skateboarding. On the other side of the skatepark was Ava, a spirited girl with a contagious laugh, who loved the thrill of pushing the boundaries on her skateboard.

Their skateboards were not just pieces of wood with wheels; they were vessels of dreams, carrying them through the twists and turns of adolescence. The local skatepark became their haven, a place where the clattering sound of wheels against concrete was a melody that spoke of freedom and self-expression.

One sunny afternoon, as Tyler and Ava prepared for their routine skate session, they noticed a poster on the community board. It announced a regional skateboarding competition, inviting all local skaters to showcase their skills and compete for the title of the town's skateboarding champion.

Excitement rippled through Tyler and Ava. The idea of showcasing their skills on a larger stage ignited a spark within them. However, they soon realized that the road to the competition was paved with challenges. As they practiced harder and attempted daring tricks, they faced falls and setbacks. But each tumble only fueled their determination to rise again.

Their determination caught the attention of a seasoned skateboarder named Tony, who had once been a rising star in the skateboarding scene. Tony offered to mentor Tyler and Ava, sharing his experiences and teaching them the nuances of advanced tricks.

Under Tony's guidance, Tyler and Ava's skills soared. The local skatepark witnessed a transformation as the duo practiced day in and day out, honing their craft. Their friendship strengthened, and their confidence blossomed like the wheels beneath their feet.

The day of the competition arrived, and the atmosphere crackled with anticipation. As Tyler and Ava stepped onto the skatepark's ramps, the cheers of the crowd blended with the rhythmic sound of their wheels. They executed flawless tricks, defying gravity and painting the air with a tapestry of daring maneuvers.

The judges were captivated by the duo's performance. Tyler's gravity-defying flips and Ava's seamless transitions between ramps left an indelible mark on the audience. The announcement echoed through the park: Tyler and Ava were crowned the town's skateboarding champions.

As they stood on the winner's podium, medals around their necks, Tyler and Ava realized that the true victory lay not in the titles but in the journey of growth, friendship, and the unyielding wheels of determination. The local skatepark, once just a place for practice, became a symbol of their triumph—a testament to the power of passion and perseverance.

And so, in the heart of their sunlit suburb, the story of Tyler and Ava, the skateboarding champions, rolled on, inspiring a new generation to carve their paths with wheels of determination.

5. Fast and Fearless Feet: Ethan and Sofia's Track and Field Adventure

Once upon a time in the vibrant town of Crestwood, where the sun kissed the rolling hills and the air buzzed with excitement, lived two inseparable friends, Ethan and Sofia. Their days were filled with laughter, games, and a shared passion for sports that echoed through the neighborhood.

Ethan, with his unruly brown hair and a perpetual twinkle in his hazel eyes, was known for his swift legs that seemed to have a life of their own. Track and field was his playground, and every sprint, every jump, was a testament to his boundless energy. Sofia, on the other hand, was a picture of grace and determination. Her fiery red hair matched her fiery spirit, and the track was where she found solace, especially when she hurdled through life's challenges.

Their journey into the world of track and field began one sunny afternoon when they stumbled upon a local track meet. The cheers of the crowd and the rhythmic pounding of spikes against the track filled the air with a contagious energy. It was in that moment, beneath the expansive blue sky, that Ethan and Sofia knew they had found their calling.

Under the watchful eye of Coach Anderson, a seasoned track and field mentor with a silver-streaked beard that told tales of countless races, the duo honed their skills. Ethan's nimble feet were molded into a force to be reckoned with, while Sofia's focused determination turned hurdles into mere stepping stones.

As the seasons changed, so did the challenges. Their journey was marked by victories and defeats, each race bringing new lessons and forging an unbreakable bond between them. Ethan's signature move, the "Blazing Bolt," a lightning-fast sprint that left competitors in awe, became a symbol of his fearless approach. Meanwhile, Sofia's "Soaring Leap" over the hurdles became a testament to her indomitable spirit.

But it wasn't just about the races. The track and field became a canvas for their friendship, where every step was a shared dance, and every jump was a leap of faith. In their pursuit of excellence, they discovered the true essence of sportsmanship—supporting each other, celebrating victories, and lifting each other up in defeat.

As the town prepared for the annual championship, Ethan and Sofia found themselves facing their most formidable opponents yet. The competition was fierce, but their determination burned brighter. In the final race, as they stood side by side, the cheers of the crowd blending into a symphony of encouragement, Ethan and Sofia knew that win or lose, they had already triumphed.

In that defining moment, as they crossed the finish line hand in hand, their fast and fearless feet had not only conquered the track but had left an indelible mark on the hearts of everyone who witnessed their extraordinary adventure. And so, in the golden glow of victory, Ethan and Sofia realized that the real treasure was not the medals around their necks but the enduring bond forged on the track and field of dreams.

6.Archery Artistry: Lily and Noah's Bullseye Quest

Once upon a time in the small town of Willowbrook, nestled between rolling hills and meandering streams, lived two inseparable friends, Lily and Noah. Lily was known for her boundless energy and creativity, while Noah was a quiet and thoughtful boy with a deep love for nature.

One sunny afternoon, Lily and Noah stumbled upon the town's archery range during the annual Willowbrook Fair. The sight of archers aiming at targets with precision fascinated them. The rhythmic twang of bowstrings and the satisfying thud as arrows hit their mark seemed like a symphony, captivating their hearts.

The fair's archery coach, Mr. Thompson, noticed the spark in Lily and Noah's eyes. With a warm smile, he invited them to try their hand at archery. Lily, ever the adventurer, was eager to accept the challenge.

Noah, though more reserved, felt a newfound curiosity bubbling within him.

Under Mr. Thompson's patient guidance, Lily and Noah learned the art of archery. They practiced tirelessly, their arrows slicing through the air, aiming for the elusive bullseye. Lily's enthusiasm and Noah's focused determination complemented each other perfectly, creating a dynamic duo on the archery range.

As weeks passed, the duo faced challenges that tested their patience and perseverance. Lily struggled with consistency, often missing the mark despite her boundless energy. Noah, on the other hand, found it difficult to unleash the power needed to propel the arrow to its target. Yet, every missed shot only fueled their determination to improve.

Their efforts caught the attention of the town, and soon, Willowbrook's first-ever Youth Archery Competition was announced. Lily and Noah, now known as the "Archery Artisans," embraced the opportunity to showcase their newfound skills.

The day of the competition arrived, with the archery range buzzing with excitement. Lily and Noah stood side by side, their bows at the ready. The crowd held its breath as the first arrow soared through the air. Lily's arrow found its mark, earning cheers from the spectators. Noah, with a calm focus, hit the bullseye with precision.

As the competition unfolded, Lily and Noah faced fierce competitors, each shot bringing them closer to the championship. Their journey wasn't just about hitting targets; it was a testament to their growth, friendship, and the power of perseverance.

In the final round, Lily and Noah faced off against each other. The tension was palpable as they aimed for the bullseye, knowing that their greatest competition was the friend standing beside them. With unwavering focus, Lily and Noah released their arrows simultaneously.

The arrows sailed through the air, and as they hit their targets, the crowd erupted into cheers. Lily's arrow grazed the edge of the bullseye, while Noah's landed dead center. In that moment, the joy on Noah's face was mirrored by the pride in Lily's eyes. The true victory wasn't in winning but in the shared journey of discovery and the bond that grew stronger with every arrow released.

As the sun dipped below the horizon, casting a warm glow over Willowbrook, Lily and Noah stood on the archery range, medals around their necks, and hearts full of accomplishment. The "Archery Artisans" had not only hit bullseyes but had also discovered the artistry of friendship and the limitless possibilities that unfold when you aim for your dreams together.

7. Soccer Squad: Mason and Lily's Teamwork Triumph

Mason couldn't believe his luck when he joined the local soccer team. The field stretched out before him, vibrant green against the backdrop of a clear blue sky. As he laced up his cleats, he couldn't shake off the nervous excitement bubbling within him.

The coach, a seasoned player named Coach Taylor, gathered the team for introductions. Among the new faces was Lily, a determined girl with a spark of enthusiasm in her eyes. Mason felt an instant connection with her, sensing a shared passion for the game.

Practice began, and Mason and Lily found themselves paired up for a passing drill. From the first kick, they discovered an incredible synergy. Mason's strong kicks complemented Lily's precise control. Coach Taylor noticed the chemistry between them and decided to make them the dynamic duo of the team.

As the soccer season unfolded, Mason and Lily faced various challenges. There were tough opponents, unexpected setbacks, and moments when victory seemed out of reach. But through it all, their teamwork shone brightly.

Off the field, Mason and Lily became inseparable friends. They spent weekends practicing in the park, refining their skills, and encouraging each other to be better. Their friendship extended beyond the soccer field, and they became true teammates in every sense of the word.

The pinnacle of their journey came during the championship game. The opposing team was formidable, with a reputation for overpowering their rivals. Mason and Lily knew they had to bring their A-game to stand a chance.

The game was intense, with both teams giving their all. Mason and Lily orchestrated plays that left the crowd in awe. As the final minutes ticked away, they found themselves in a tiebreaker situation. It all came down to one decisive moment.

In a brilliant display of coordination, Mason passed the ball to Lily, who skillfully maneuvered through the opposing defenders. With a swift kick, she sent the ball soaring into the net, securing the championship for their team. The crowd erupted in cheers as Mason and Lily embraced, celebrating not just a victory on the field but a triumph of teamwork and friendship.

Their journey became an inspiration to the entire community. The local newspaper featured their story, and young soccer enthusiasts looked up to Mason and Lily as role models. The soccer squad, once just a team, had transformed into a tight-knit family bonded by the joy of the game and the spirit of teamwork.

And so, as the sun set on the championship day, Mason and Lily reveled in the realization that true victory goes beyond scoreboards—it's found in the bonds of friendship and the shared love for the beautiful game of soccer.

8. Sailing Dreams Ahoy: Carter and Mia's Seafaring Adventure

Once upon a time in the coastal town of Harbor Haven, two young friends, Carter and Mia, discovered a shared love for the vast expanse of the sea. Their connection to the ocean wasn't just a fascination; it was a calling that would set them on an extraordinary seafaring adventure.

Carter, with his unruly sandy hair and a perpetual twinkle in his blue eyes, grew up surrounded by the salty breeze of the ocean. His family owned a small sailing shop, and he spent countless hours helping his father repair sails and polish boat decks. Mia, on the other hand, was a recent transplant to Harbor Haven. Her family moved from a bustling city to the serene coastal town, seeking a slower pace of life.

The duo met one sunny afternoon when Mia was exploring the marina. Intrigued by the colorful sails and the rhythmic creaking of the boats, she couldn't help but feel a magnetic pull toward the water. It was there, amidst the masts and the seagull symphony, that she encountered Carter.

Carter, always eager to share his love for sailing, offered Mia a tour of his family's sailboat—the Sea Serenity. As the sails billowed in the wind, he explained the nuances of tacking and jibing, the art of navigating the open sea. Mia's eyes sparkled with newfound excitement, and a friendship was born.

The two friends spent their weekends exploring hidden coves, racing against the wind, and chasing sunsets on the horizon. Mia, with her knack for navigation, quickly became an integral part of the sailing duo. Carter admired her fearlessness and the way she embraced every challenge the sea threw their way.

One day, as they were navigating through a particularly challenging stretch of water, a sudden squall struck. The wind howled, and the waves rose like towering giants. The Sea Serenity pitched and rolled, challenging even the most seasoned sailors. Yet, Carter and Mia faced the tempest head-on, their bond and determination unwavering.

As they weathered the storm, Carter and Mia discovered not only the resilience of their friendship but also the indomitable spirit within themselves. Their seafaring adventure became a metaphor for life's challenges—sometimes unpredictable and tumultuous, yet always navigable with courage and camaraderie.

The story of Carter and Mia's sailing dreams unfolded against the backdrop of breathtaking sunsets, playful dolphins, and the ever-changing hues of the sea. It became a testament to the transformative power of shared passions, the strength found in facing challenges together, and the joy of discovering one's true self on the open waters.

And so, with each sail unfurled and every wave conquered, Carter and Mia's seafaring adventure continued, leaving a trail of inspiration for young readers to follow their dreams, embrace challenges, and set sail into the vast ocean of possibilities that life offers.

9. Home Run Harmony: Owen, Emma, and the Melodies of Baseball

Once upon a sun-drenched summer in the vibrant town of Harmonyville, two inseparable friends, Owen and Emma, discovered the magical intersection of baseball and music.

Owen, with his unruly mop of brown hair and a perpetual baseball cap perched on his head, was the heart and soul of Harmonyville's little league team. His agile moves on the baseball diamond were matched only by his infectious laughter that echoed through the stands during every game.

Emma, on the other hand, was a melody in motion. With her bright blue eyes and a guitar always in tow, she was known as the town's young songbird. From busking on the street corners to serenading at local events, Emma's music had the power to bring smiles to every face in Harmonyville.

One sunny afternoon, as Owen was practicing his swings at the local baseball field, Emma decided to surprise him with an impromptu performance. Sitting on the bleachers with her guitar, she strummed a cheerful tune that seemed to dance with the rhythm of Owen's swings.

The magic was instant. The crack of the bat synchronized seamlessly with Emma's chords, creating a harmonious blend that captivated everyone at the field. The duo unintentionally became the talk of the town, and soon enough, the entire community gathered to witness this unique collaboration of sports and music.

Inspired by the positive response, Owen and Emma decided to bring their "Home Run Harmony" to every game. Emma's guitar melodies became the unofficial soundtrack of the baseball season, turning each match into a festive celebration. The once ordinary little league games transformed into extraordinary events, drawing families and friends from neighboring towns.

As their fame spread, so did the sense of community in Harmonyville. The local businesses began sponsoring the games, and the town's spirit soared to new heights. Owen's home runs and Emma's harmonies became synonymous with unity, friendship, and the sheer joy of small-town life.

One fateful evening, as the sun dipped below the horizon, casting a warm glow over the baseball field, Owen hit a colossal home run that sailed over the fence. The crowd erupted into cheers, and Emma strummed a triumphant chord, creating a moment that would be etched in Harmonyville's history.

"Home Run Harmony" became more than just a local phenomenon—it became a symbol of the magic that happens when passions collide. Owen and Emma's story continues to inspire young athletes and musicians, reminding them that true greatness is found not just in individual achievements but in the harmonious blend of shared dreams.

And so, in the heart of Harmonyville, the echoes of baseballs meeting bats and guitars strumming chords continue to create a melody that celebrates the timeless spirit of friendship, sportsmanship, and the magic that happens when dreams harmonize.

10. Icebound Trailblazers: Riley and Harper's Figure Skating Symphony

In the heart of Millington Falls, where winters painted the landscape in blankets of pristine white, lived two kindred spirits, Riley and Harper. The town, known for its frozen lakes and snow-kissed trees, became the perfect stage for their unique journey into the world of figure skating.

Riley, with her vibrant red hair and infectious laughter, had dreamed of gliding across the ice since she first stepped onto the frozen pond behind her house. Harper, with her determination and a penchant for snowboarding down the steepest slopes, found an unexpected allure in the graceful artistry of figure skating.

Their paths converged at the Millington Falls Skating Rink, a small haven where dreams took flight on glistening ice. Under the tutelage of Coach Victoria, an elegant former figure skater with a heart full of passion, Riley and Harper began their training.

The early days were filled with wobbles and tumbles, as the duo traded snowboards for skates, embracing the challenges with unwavering determination. As they practiced their first twirls and jumps, the icy surface beneath them transformed into a canvas where their dreams would take shape.

The town soon buzzed with excitement as news of the trailblazing pair spread. The Millington Falls Figure Skating Symphony was born, an ensemble of two, crafting a unique melody with every pirouette and leap. Riley's fiery spirit and Harper's adventurous flair created a harmonious blend that captivated the hearts of everyone who witnessed their performances.

As the winter competitions approached, Riley and Harper faced not only the pressure of perfecting their routines but also the skepticism of those who doubted their unconventional pairing. Undeterred, the two friends leaned on each other, finding strength in their shared passion for figure skating.

The day of the Millington Falls Winter Skating Championship arrived, casting a magical aura over the rink. Riley and Harper, dressed in shimmering costumes that mirrored the glistening snowflakes around them, took to the ice with a confidence that spoke volumes. Their routine unfolded like a symphony, a seamless fusion of grace and daring moves that left the audience in awe.

The judges, initially skeptical, were swept away by the magic created by Riley and Harper. The applause echoed through the rink as the duo received a standing ovation, their triumph transcending the confines of a mere competition.

The Millington Falls Figure Skating Symphony had not only triumphed on the ice but had also shattered stereotypes, proving that passion knows no boundaries and that a harmonious melody can emerge from the most unexpected duet.

As the snow continued to fall in Millington Falls, the legacy of Riley and Harper lived on. The skating rink became a symbol of dreams realized, and the figure skating symphony echoed in the hearts of all who dared to defy convention and dance to the rhythm of their own dreams.

11. Skate Park Symphony: Logan and Jordan's Boarding Bliss

Once upon a sunlit town nestled between rolling hills, there stood a skate park, the beating heart of adrenaline and freedom. It was here that two inseparable friends, Logan and Jordan, discovered the rhythm of their own unique symphony—one composed of wheels against concrete, laughter echoing through ramps, and the unmistakable pulse of skateboards soaring through the air.

Logan, with his unruly mop of sun-kissed hair and a perpetual grin, had a knack for turning the simplest trick into a work of art. Jordan, on the other hand, was the quiet maestro of the skate park, navigating the terrain with a grace that seemed almost otherworldly. Together, they formed an extraordinary duo, their boards dancing to a melody only they could hear.

The skate park, a canvas of concrete curves and ramps, became the backdrop for Logan and Jordan's daily escapades. From sunrise to sunset, they pushed each other to new heights, their laughter resonating like a carefree melody in the air. But beneath the surface of their joyous routines, a deeper connection thrived—one built on shared dreams and unspoken understanding.

One fateful day, a regional skateboarding competition was announced, drawing skaters from all corners of the town. The news ignited a spark in Logan and Jordan's hearts. It was a chance to showcase their unique style, to let their boards become instruments in the grand symphony of skateboarding.

As the competition day approached, Logan and Jordan spent every waking moment perfecting their routine. Their days became a blur of sunsets at the skate park, practicing under the glow of flickering streetlights. The anticipation of the event brought a mixture of excitement and nerves, but Logan and Jordan faced the challenge with unwavering determination.

The morning of the competition arrived, and the skate park buzzed with energy. Spectators gathered around the ramps, eager to witness the talents of the local skaters. Logan and Jordan, dressed in matching custom-designed skate gear, felt the weight of the moment but also the surge of adrenaline that came with it.

The announcer's voice echoed through the park as Logan and Jordan took their positions at the starting line. The first notes of their skating symphony began with a synchronized drop-in, their boards seamlessly carving through the transitions. From kickflips to ollies, the duo wove a tapestry of tricks that left the audience in awe.

Their routine reached its crescendo as they executed a gravity-defying trick, a move they had mastered in secret. The crowd erupted in cheers, and the judges nodded in approval. In that moment, Logan and Jordan realized they had not only shared their passion with the world but had also created a skateboarding legacy in their small town.

As the sun dipped below the horizon, casting long shadows over the skate park, Logan and Jordan stood side by side, catching their breath. Their journey from carefree skaters to local legends was a testament to the power of friendship, shared dreams, and the pure joy found in the symphony of skateboarding.

And so, as the stars emerged in the night sky, Logan and Jordan continued to skate beneath the silver glow, their boards creating a melody that resonated far beyond the borders of their small town—the Skate Park Symphony that echoed in the hearts of every aspiring skateboarder who dared to dream.

12. Dribble and Dream: Mia and Dylan's Hoop Dreams

Once upon a time in the bustling city of Brookville, Mia and Dylan, two inseparable friends with an unyielding passion for basketball, embarked on a journey that would not only transform their lives but also leave an indelible mark on their community.

Mia, a spirited and determined young girl with a love for dribbling and shooting hoops, discovered her affinity for basketball at a local community center. Her eyes sparkled with excitement as she witnessed her first slam dunk, and from that moment on, Mia knew that basketball would be more than just a game for her; it would be a way of life.

Dylan, her best friend and partner in all adventures, was quick to catch on to Mia's infectious enthusiasm for the sport. Tall and lanky, Dylan possessed a natural talent for the game. The duo spent countless afternoons on the worn-out basketball court in the heart of their neighborhood, practicing layups, perfecting jump shots, and dreaming of the day they would hear the roar of the crowd as they scored the winning points.

Their dreams took flight when Coach Johnson, a former professional basketball player turned mentor, noticed their dedication and potential during a local tournament. Impressed by their skills and inspired by their unwavering friendship, Coach Johnson invited Mia and Dylan to join the newly formed Brookville Youth Basketball Team.

As part of the team, Mia and Dylan faced challenges that tested their determination. Mia, being one of the few girls on the team, encountered skepticism and doubters who questioned her abilities. However, she silenced them with her lightning-quick crossovers and precision three-pointers. Dylan, on the other hand, grappled with self-doubt as he faced taller and more experienced opponents. Yet, with Mia by his side, he found the courage to rise above the challenges.

The Brookville Youth Basketball Team embarked on a thrilling journey of tournaments, victories, and defeats. Mia and Dylan's unique playing styles complemented each other, and their synergy on the court became the talk of the town. As their friendship deepened, so did their understanding of the game and their shared dream of making it to the regional championships.

Amidst the adrenaline-pumping games and nail-biting finishes, Mia and Dylan discovered the true essence of basketball: teamwork, resilience, and the pursuit of a common goal. With every dribble, they proved that gender and size were no barriers to success on the basketball court.

The climax of their journey arrived on a bright Saturday afternoon in the championship game against their arch-rivals, the Brookville Thunderbolts. The entire community gathered to witness the showdown, and the atmosphere was charged with anticipation. In the final minutes of the game, with the score tied, Mia and Dylan executed a play they had practiced countless times on their neighborhood court. The ball danced between them, weaving through the opposing defense, and in the last seconds, Mia took the shot that echoed through the ages—a perfect swish.

The cheers of the crowd were deafening as Mia and Dylan celebrated their victory. The dreams they had dribbled and practiced for had become a reality. The championship trophy sparkled in the hands of the Brookville Youth Basketball Team, and Mia and Dylan's hoop dreams had not only come true but had also become an inspiration for aspiring young players in Brookville.

From that day forward, the story of Mia and Dylan's hoop dreams became a legend in their community. The worn-out basketball court witnessed the dreams of many young athletes who, just like Mia and Dylan, aspired to dribble and dream their way to success. And so, in the heart of Brookville, the echoes of basketballs bouncing and dreams soaring filled the air, a testament to the enduring spirit of two friends who dared to dream beyond the bounds of the court.

13. Cliffhanger Climbers: Sierra and Justin's Rock Climbing Thrills

Once upon a time, in the picturesque town of Summitville, nestled between majestic mountains and lush forests, lived two adventurous souls named Sierra and Justin. Their shared love for the outdoors and thrill-seeking activities drew them together, forming a friendship as strong as the granite cliffs that surrounded their quaint town.

Sierra, with her sun-kissed hair and a perpetual spark of curiosity in her eyes, spent her childhood exploring the hills that enveloped Summitville. Her favorite pastime was climbing trees, a passion that would soon evolve into a much more daring pursuit. Justin, on the other hand, moved to Summitville from the bustling city, seeking a different rhythm in life. His nimble fingers and agile frame hinted at a natural talent for climbing, a skill he was yet to discover.

The turning point in Sierra and Justin's lives came one sunny afternoon when they stumbled upon the town's rock climbing gym, aptly named "Summit Ascent." The moment they set foot inside, the scent of chalk and the distant echoes of climbers filled the air. Sierra's eyes widened with excitement, and Justin's heart raced at the prospect of a new adventure.

Under the watchful eye of Coach Elena, a seasoned climber and the heart of Summit Ascent, Sierra and Justin began their rock climbing journey. The gym's walls, adorned with colorful holds and routes of varying difficulty, became their playground. Each ascent was a challenge, a puzzle to be solved with strength, technique, and a dash of fearlessness.

Sierra's determination was evident as she fearlessly tackled each route, her fingers gripping the holds with unwavering tenacity. She embraced the vertical terrain, finding solace in the heights that once intimidated her. Justin, though new to the sport, showcased a natural aptitude for climbing. With each climb, he discovered the strength within himself and a newfound passion for the vertical world.

As Sierra and Justin's skills evolved, Coach Elena saw the potential for something greater. She proposed a daring adventure: to conquer the town's iconic cliff, a sheer rock face that loomed above Summitville. Known as "Eagle's Perch," the cliff held a mystique that captivated the entire community.

The news of Sierra and Justin attempting Eagle's Perch spread like wildfire, creating a buzz of anticipation in Summitville. Friends, family, and fellow climbers rallied around them, offering support and encouragement. The climbing duo, now known as the "Cliffhanger Climbers," prepared for their most significant ascent yet.

The day arrived, the sun painting the sky in hues of orange and pink as Sierra and Justin stood at the base of Eagle's Perch. The air was charged with excitement and nerves, but their determination drowned out any doubts. With harnesses secured and ropes in place, they began their ascent.

As they climbed higher, the town below transformed into a miniature landscape. The wind whispered tales of triumph, and the distant cheers from supporters echoed through the canyon. Sierra and Justin's synchronized movements painted a portrait of resilience, showcasing the unbreakable bond forged through their climbing adventures.

Finally, they reached the summit, a moment frozen in time. The panoramic view from Eagle's Perch unveiled the beauty of Summitville and the vast possibilities that stretched beyond. Sierra and Justin, breathless and triumphant, exchanged a glance that spoke volumes—proof that with determination, support, and a touch of courage, even the most challenging cliffs could be conquered.

The Cliffhanger Climbers became local legends, inspiring a new generation of adventurers in Summitville. Sierra and Justin continued exploring the heights, knowing that the journey, with all its twists and turns, was the real thrill of the climb. And so, the sun continued to set over the mountains, casting long shadows on the cliffs that held the stories of Sierra, Justin, and the town that celebrated their daring spirit.

14. Goalkeeper's Grace: Aidan and Zoe's Soccer Saves

In the vibrant town of Crestwood, where soccer fields echoed with cheers and the spirit of competition, two young souls, Aidan and Zoe, found themselves drawn to the goalpost, driven by a shared passion for soccer.

Aidan, with his unruly mop of brown hair and a perpetual grin, had an innate love for the game. His eyes lit up with excitement every time the ball was at his feet. Zoe, on the other hand, possessed a quiet determination beneath her curly auburn locks. She had a unique knack for reading the game, anticipating moves with an almost telepathic precision.

Their friendship began on the dusty fields of Crestwood Elementary School, where they were assigned to the same soccer team. As fate would have it, Aidan was the aspiring goalkeeper, and Zoe was the steadfast defender by his side. Their synergy on the field was undeniable from the start.

Coach Thompson, an enthusiastic supporter of young talent, noticed the duo's potential. With a knowing smile, he appointed Aidan as the official goalkeeper and Zoe as his trusted defender. Their bond deepened as they practiced tirelessly, honing their skills after school and on weekends.

The town's annual soccer tournament, "Crestwood Cup," was fast approaching, and excitement buzzed through the air. Aidan and Zoe were determined to make a mark. Little did they know that their defining moment would come in the championship match against their arch-rivals, the Crestview Cyclones.

The game was intense, with both teams locked in a fierce battle. Aidan's goalkeeping skills were put to the test as the Cyclones launched one attack after another. Zoe, agile and strategic, thwarted opponent after opponent, ensuring the ball stayed as far away from their goal as possible.

As the final minutes ticked away, the score tied at 1-1, Crestwood had one last chance. The Cyclones, with a sudden surge of energy, launched a powerful shot towards the goal. Aidan, displaying a grace beyond his years, leaped and deflected the ball with a spectacular save.

The crowd erupted into cheers, but the game wasn't over. In the closing moments, Crestwood secured a corner kick. With bated breath, Zoe positioned herself for the crucial play. The ball soared into the penalty area, and with a swift header, she directed it away from danger.

The referee's whistle signaled the end of the game. Aidan and Zoe, exhausted but elated, were lifted on their teammates' shoulders. Crestwood had won the "Crestwood Cup," and the dynamic duo's soccer saves had etched their names in the town's history.

Their journey from passionate players to celebrated heroes taught Crestwood, and especially the young aspiring athletes, that true victory isn't just about scoring goals; it's about unwavering teamwork, indomitable spirit, and the grace that comes from the heart of the game. As the sun set on the Crestwood Cup, Aidan and Zoe shared a triumphant moment, realizing that sometimes, saving goals was about much more than just blocking shots—it was about saving dreams and creating memories that would last a lifetime.

15. Judo Journeys: Hannah and Liam's Martial Arts Adventure

Once upon a time in the quiet town of Crestwood, nestled between rolling hills and ancient forests, lived two friends, Hannah and Liam. Their bond was as strong as the mountains that surrounded their town, and their curiosity was as boundless as the starry night sky.

Hannah, with her fiery red hair and determined spirit, had always been fascinated by the art of Judo. The rhythmic movements, the discipline, and the philosophy behind it captured her imagination. Liam, on the other hand, was a more reserved soul with a heart full of courage. He admired Hannah's passion for Judo and decided to embark on a martial arts adventure together.

Their journey began one crisp autumn afternoon when they stumbled upon the Crestwood Martial Arts Dojo, a quaint building at the edge of town with a weathered wooden sign that swung gently in the breeze. Intrigued, they stepped inside, where the scent of polished wood and the echoes of disciplined movements filled the air.

The sensei, a wise and patient man named Master Takashi, welcomed them with a warm smile. He sensed the spark of determination in their eyes and agreed to take them under his wing. And so, Hannah and Liam's Judo journey commenced.

The dojo became a second home for the duo. The rhythmic slaps of the mat, the laughter echoing through the hall, and the lessons of respect and self-discipline surrounded them. Master Takashi guided them through the art of falling gracefully, the precise techniques of throws, and the importance of mental fortitude.

As weeks turned into months, Hannah and Liam progressed from white belts to yellow, then orange, with each new belt representing a milestone in their growth. Their friendship strengthened as they practiced together, learned from each other, and faced challenges with unwavering support.

One day, Master Takashi announced the upcoming regional Judo tournament, a chance for his students to showcase their skills and sportsmanship. The excitement in the dojo was palpable, and Hannah and Liam eagerly signed up. Training intensified as the tournament drew near, and the two friends pushed each other to new heights.

The day of the tournament arrived, and Crestwood's dojo was abuzz with energy. Hannah and Liam stepped onto the mat, their hearts pounding with a mix of nerves and determination. The matches were fierce, but the two friends executed their throws with precision, showcasing the artistry they had learned.

In the final round, Hannah found herself facing a formidable opponent. The air was tense as the match unfolded. With a swift movement, Hannah executed a perfect throw, earning her victory and a standing ovation from the crowd. Liam, watching with pride, knew their Judo journey had reached a defining moment.

As the sun set on Crestwood, casting a warm glow over the dojo, Master Takashi congratulated Hannah and Liam on their achievements. Their martial arts adventure had not only forged their bodies into formidable Judokas but had also shaped their characters, instilling values of respect, perseverance, and camaraderie.

And so, in the quiet town of Crestwood, where the mountains stood tall and the forests whispered ancient tales, two friends, Hannah and Liam, continued their Judo journeys, their spirits forever entwined in the artful dance of martial arts and friendship.

16. Soccer Science Wonders: Olivia and Ethan's Kickin' Experiments

Once upon a time in the sunny town of Crestwood, two adventurous young minds, Olivia and Ethan, found themselves at the heart of an incredible soccer journey that blended the excitement of the field with the wonders of science.

Olivia, with her fiery red hair and a soccer ball always at her feet, was known for her swift moves and dazzling footwork. Ethan, her best friend and partner in crime, was a tech whiz with a passion for experiments and discoveries. Together, they were an unstoppable duo with an insatiable curiosity for the game they loved.

One sunny afternoon, as they kicked the ball around in the neighborhood park, an idea sparked in Ethan's mind. "What if we combine soccer with science?" he exclaimed, eyes gleaming with excitement. Olivia, always up for an adventure, was immediately intrigued.

Their first experiment involved attaching small sensors to Olivia's soccer shoes to measure the force of her kicks. With the help of Ethan's homemade invention, they discovered the correlation between the power of Olivia's kicks and the distance the ball traveled. The pair couldn't contain their excitement as they witnessed science unraveling the mysteries of soccer right before their eyes.

As word spread about Olivia and Ethan's kickin' experiments, the local soccer coach, Coach Anderson, took notice. Intrigued by the innovative approach, Coach invited the dynamic duo to join the Crestwood Strikers, the town's youth soccer team. The team was preparing for the upcoming championship, and Coach believed Olivia and Ethan's scientific insights could give them an edge.

Embracing the challenge, Olivia and Ethan delved deeper into their experiments. They explored the aerodynamics of soccer balls, studied the impact of different surfaces on ball movement, and even experimented with the perfect angle for scoring goals. Each discovery brought them closer to unraveling the secrets that could make them champions on the field.

Their journey wasn't without hurdles. As the championship day approached, the Crestwood Strikers faced a formidable opponent, the Rivertown Rovers. The rival team, known for their skillful plays, seemed unbeatable. Doubt crept into Olivia and Ethan's minds, but their belief in the power of science and teamwork kept them going.

On the day of the championship, the field buzzed with anticipation. The Crestwood Strikers, armed with their newfound knowledge, faced the Rivertown Rovers in a match that would go down in history. Olivia, with her swift kicks, and Ethan, with his strategic insights, led the team with determination.

The game unfolded with breathtaking moments of skill, teamwork, and the occasional surprise from Olivia and Ethan's scientific strategies. As the final whistle blew, the scoreboard displayed a tied score: 2-2. The Crestwood Strikers had held their ground against the formidable Rivertown Rovers.

In the nail-biting penalty shootout that followed, Olivia stepped up with a confident smile. She remembered the lessons learned through their kickin' experiments. With a powerful kick, she scored the winning goal, securing victory for the Crestwood Strikers.

The town erupted in cheers as Olivia and Ethan's scientific approach to soccer not only made them champions but also inspired a newfound love for the beautiful game blended with the wonders of science. The soccer field became a place where passion, curiosity, and teamwork converged to create an unforgettable tale of triumph and discovery. And so, in the heart of Crestwood, the legacy of Soccer Science Wonders lived on, inspiring generations of young athletes to kick off their own adventures in the world of soccer and science.

17. Ballet and Balance: Isabella and Noah's Dance Delight

Once upon a time, in the vibrant city of Grandridge, two young souls, Isabella and Noah, discovered the enchanting world of ballet. They were drawn together by a shared passion for the delicate art form, a world where every movement told a story, and where balance was not just a physical feat but a metaphor for life.

Isabella, with her flowing brown hair and grace that seemed to defy gravity, had always been fascinated by the beauty and elegance of ballet. Noah, a spirited and energetic boy with a flair for rhythm, found himself captivated by the artistry of dance after attending a performance with his family.

Their paths converged at the Grandridge School of Ballet, a place where dreams pirouetted into reality. Isabella and Noah, both beginners in the world of ballet, found themselves in the same introductory class. Mrs. Henderson, the seasoned ballet instructor with a warmth that matched her passion for dance, welcomed them with open arms.

From the first plié to the grand jeté, Isabella and Noah embraced the challenges of learning ballet. They stumbled and laughed together, their friendship blossoming in the mirrored studio surrounded by the soft strains of classical music. Mrs. Henderson recognized the unique energy they brought to the studio, a perfect blend of determination and joy.

As the days turned into weeks, and the weeks into months, Isabella and Noah discovered the importance of balance not just in their dance routines but in their lives. Ballet, it seemed, was teaching them lessons beyond the studio. Isabella learned to balance her perfectionism with self-compassion, while Noah discovered the harmony between discipline and spontaneity.

Their journey reached a crescendo when the Grandridge Ballet School announced its annual recital. The theme was "Harmony in Motion," and each dancer was encouraged to express their unique style. Isabella and Noah decided to choreograph their own duet, a blend of classical ballet and contemporary movements that reflected their friendship and individual growth.

Rehearsals became a sacred space where they explored their choreography, and the studio echoed with the music of their collaboration. Mrs. Henderson, with a twinkle in her eye, encouraged their creativity, recognizing the spark of something extraordinary in their performance.

The night of the recital arrived, the stage adorned with soft lights and the air humming with anticipation. Isabella, in a sea of pale pink, and Noah, in a tailored black suit, stood backstage, nerves and excitement intertwining. As the curtain rose, their dance unfolded—a mesmerizing tapestry of balance, grace, and friendship.

The audience was spellbound as Isabella and Noah moved in unison, telling a story that transcended the confines of the stage. Each pirouette and arabesque painted a picture of two souls finding harmony, both in dance and in life. The applause that followed was thunderous, a celebration of not just their performance but the journey that led them to that moment.

After the recital, Isabella and Noah stood hand in hand, their hearts brimming with gratitude. Ballet had brought them together, and through its delicate movements, they had discovered a lifelong friendship and the beauty of balance in every step they took.

And so, in the city of Grandridge, the echoes of "Ballet and Balance" continued, a timeless melody that danced through the hearts of Isabella, Noah, and all who witnessed their enchanting journey into the world of dance delight.

18. Victory Garden Run: Ava, Mason, and the Joy of Gardening

Once upon a time, in a quaint little town nestled between rolling hills and green meadows, lived two spirited friends named Ava and Mason. Their story unfolded in the warm embrace of nature, where the scent of blooming flowers and the gentle rustle of leaves set the backdrop for their remarkable adventure.

Ava, with her vibrant red hair and a perpetual twinkle in her green eyes, lived in a charming cottage surrounded by a kaleidoscope of flowers. Mason, a freckled boy with an infectious grin, resided just a stone's throw away, in a cozy house shaded by a towering oak tree.

One sunny afternoon, as the duo strolled through their neighborhood, they stumbled upon a neglected piece of land, overrun by weeds and wildflowers. Inspired by a shared love for nature, Ava and Mason decided to transform this forgotten space into a beautiful garden—a haven for plants, animals, and their entire community.

Equipped with shovels, seeds, and unwavering determination, the dynamic duo began their gardening escapade. Mason, with his sturdy hands, tilled the soil, while Ava, armed with a rainbow of seeds, brought life back to the forgotten earth. Together, they planted sunflowers that reached for the sky, tomatoes that blushed with ripeness, and herbs that perfumed the air.

Their garden became a sanctuary, attracting butterflies, bees, and the curious noses of neighboring bunnies. As word spread about Ava and Mason's gardening marvel, more hands joined in. The once-neglected plot transformed into a vibrant tapestry of colors and scents, uniting the community in a shared love for nature.

But Ava and Mason envisioned more than just a beautiful garden—they dreamt of a race, a celebration of their achievements and the joy that bloomed with each seed. And so, the "Victory Garden Run" was born—a race through the twists and turns of their garden, where the finish line was adorned with the sweetest blossoms and the promise of shared triumph.

On the day of the race, the sun shone brightly, casting a golden glow over the garden. Friends, families, and fellow garden enthusiasts gathered to witness the spectacle. Ava and Mason, wearing matching gardening gloves and determined expressions, stood side by side at the starting line.

The race began with a burst of laughter and the patter of eager feet on the soft soil. Ava and Mason led the way, sprinting past the sunflowers and leaping over the beds of fragrant lavender. The air was filled with cheers and the melodious hum of bees, adding to the festive atmosphere.

As they neared the finish line, Ava and Mason clasped hands, crossing together in a celebration of friendship, community, and the triumph of their gardening endeavor. The Victory Garden Run became an annual tradition, a reminder that even the smallest seeds of kindness and determination could grow into something extraordinary.

The garden, now a vibrant symbol of unity, continued to flourish, echoing the laughter and camaraderie that had blossomed within its bounds. Ava and Mason's story became a cherished tale in their town, inspiring generations to come to find joy in the simple act of planting seeds, nurturing friendships, and celebrating the victories that bloom along the way. And so, in the heart of the little town, the Victory Garden thrived as a testament to the enduring magic of Ava, Mason, and the joy of gardening.

19. Speedy Sprinters: Riley, Sophia, and the Race to Success

Once upon a time in the bustling town of Brooksville, two young friends, Riley and Sophia, discovered their shared love for running. Their small town was known for its vibrant community spirit, and every year, the Brooksville Annual Kids' Marathon became the highlight event that brought the community together. Riley and Sophia dreamt of not only participating but winning the race and leaving their mark on the town's history.

Riley, a spirited and determined girl with a shock of red hair, had always been the fastest in her class. She lived next door to the town's retired track coach, Coach Miller, who saw potential in her from a young age. Coach Miller, fondly known as 'Coach M,' often observed Riley's lightning-fast sprints during her playtime in the backyard. One day, he approached her and offered to train her for the upcoming marathon.

On the other side of town lived Sophia, a quiet yet incredibly resilient girl with a passion for numbers. Her analytical mind made her a strategic thinker, and she had always been intrigued by the science behind running. Sophia's dad, a former marathon runner himself, recognized her potential and encouraged her to join the town's running club.

As the two friends started training, their differences became their strengths. Riley's speed and Coach M's guidance, combined with Sophia's analytical approach and her dad's marathon wisdom, created an unstoppable duo. The town took notice, and soon enough, the entire community rallied behind Riley and Sophia, sensing something extraordinary was in the making.

The day of the Brooksville Annual Kids' Marathon arrived, and the excitement in the air was palpable. The route wound through the town's charming streets, parks, and scenic spots. Riley and Sophia, donned in their vibrant running gear, stood at the starting line with a mix of nervousness and determination.

As the starting horn blared, Riley shot off like an arrow, her feet barely touching the ground. Sophia, with calculated grace, maintained a steady pace beside her. The townspeople cheered as the duo led the pack, their friendship and competitive spirit creating an electrifying atmosphere.

The race proved challenging, with unexpected twists and turns, mirroring the journey of life itself. Riley and Sophia faced obstacles but pressed on, their resilience shining through. The finish line drew near, and as they sprinted side by side, the townspeople erupted in cheers, recognizing that the true victory lay in the camaraderie and shared success of their community.

Riley and Sophia crossed the finish line together, arms raised in triumph. The race had not only forged their paths to success but had also united the town in a celebration of friendship, perseverance, and the pursuit of dreams.

In the end, Speedy Sprinters Riley and Sophia discovered that success wasn't just about winning; it was about the journey, the bonds forged, and the inspiration they imparted to their community. The Brooksville Annual Kids' Marathon became a symbol of unity, reminding everyone that with determination, support, and a dash of friendly competition, every participant could be a winner in their own right.

20. Cycling with Courage: Maya and Carter's Biking Bliss

In the quaint town of Evergreen Valley, nestled between rolling hills and meandering streams, there lived two adventurous souls named Maya and Carter. From the earliest age, the duo shared a profound love for the thrill of cycling, with every ride symbolizing a journey into the unknown and a chance to discover the hidden wonders of their picturesque surroundings.

Maya, with her fiery red hair and an infectious enthusiasm for life, was known for her unyielding determination and unwavering spirit. Carter, her closest friend since kindergarten, had a heart as big as the mountains that surrounded their town. With his perpetually messy brown hair and a perpetual twinkle in his eyes, he was the perfect companion for Maya's cycling escapades.

One sunny afternoon, as the wind whispered through the trees and the promise of adventure hung in the air, Maya and Carter decided it was time for a new biking challenge. They had conquered every trail in Evergreen Valley, and a map unfolded before them, revealing the rugged path of Mount Horizon—an unexplored and, to some, intimidating trail.

Undeterred, the pair geared up with their helmets, backpacks, and their trusty mountain bikes. They pedaled away from the familiar streets, eager to embrace the unknown. The initial stretch was a gentle ascent, with wildflowers lining the sides of the trail. Maya and Carter laughed and chatted as they rode, their bikes creating a rhythmic harmony with nature.

As they approached the base of Mount Horizon, the terrain became steeper, and the trail more challenging. But Maya's courage and Carter's encouragement fueled their determination. They navigated hairpin turns, crossed babbling brooks, and pedaled through dense forests. The ascent was grueling, but with every push of the pedal, they felt a surge of accomplishment.

As they neared the summit, the view unfolded like a breathtaking canvas. The entire valley lay below them, bathed in the warm glow of the setting sun. Exhausted but elated, Maya and Carter marveled at the beauty around them. The journey had not only been physical but a testament to their friendship, resilience, and the bliss that comes from facing challenges head-on.

The descent was a thrilling rush of wind and adrenaline. Downhill, they weaved through the trails, their bikes skimming over rocks and roots.

Laughter echoed through the mountains as they embraced the freedom of the ride. The sunset painted the sky in hues of orange and pink, and the duo coasted back into Evergreen Valley with a profound sense of accomplishment.

Maya and Carter's biking bliss became a legendary tale in Evergreen Valley, inspiring other young adventurers to embark on their own journeys of courage and discovery. The bond forged on Mount Horizon and the joy found in the challenges of the trail solidified their friendship, creating memories that would last a lifetime in the heart of Evergreen Valley.

21. Chess Champions: Alex and Emma's Checkmate Chronicles

Once upon a time in the quiet town of Brooksville, where cobblestone streets wound their way around charming cottages and towering oak trees, lived two young friends named Alex and Emma. Despite their love for the town's tranquility, there was a fierce passion burning within them – a passion for chess.

The duo discovered the enigmatic world of chess in the town's community center. Nestled in the heart of Brooksville, the community center became a haven for youngsters seeking intellectual challenges and strategic pursuits. Alex, with his unruly mop of brown hair and a perpetual twinkle of curiosity in his hazel eyes, was an expert at maneuvering the chess pieces with unmatched precision. Emma, with her fiery red curls and a keen intellect, was known for her strategic brilliance that often left opponents in awe.

Their journey into the world of chess began when Mr. Higgins, a wise old gentleman with a penchant for mentoring young minds, noticed their potential during a casual game in the community center. Mr. Higgins, a retired chess grandmaster, recognized the spark in Alex and Emma's eyes – a spark that indicated a deep understanding of the game and an unquenchable thirst for knowledge.

Under Mr. Higgins' wise tutelage, Alex and Emma embarked on a thrilling adventure into the realm of competitive chess. The town of Brooksville buzzed with excitement as news of their growing prowess spread like wildfire. The local chess club, once a quiet gathering of enthusiasts, transformed into a vibrant hub of strategic battles and intellectual camaraderie.

As the seasons changed, so did Alex and Emma. Their passion for chess deepened, evolving from friendly games at the community center to intense battles in regional championships. The dynamics of their friendship also evolved; each match, win or lose, brought them closer, and they reveled in the intellectual dance that chess offered.

The pinnacle of their chess journey came when Brooksville hosted the prestigious National Junior Chess Championship. Alex and Emma, now recognized as Chess Champions in the town, faced competitors from across the country. The air was thick with anticipation as the duo entered the grand hall, adorned with chess boards of all sizes and the unmistakable scent of excitement.

Match after match, Alex and Emma displayed not only their mastery of the game but also their unwavering sportsmanship. Whether checkmating opponents with swift moves or graciously accepting defeat, they became the embodiment of the true spirit of chess – a game that transcends victories and defeats, teaching lessons of strategy, resilience, and respect.

The grand finale approached, and it was clear that destiny had woven a tale of rivalry between Alex and Emma. The entire town gathered to witness the Checkmate Chronicles unfold. As the tension reached its zenith, the two friends engaged in a riveting match, each move a carefully calculated step towards victory.

In the end, with the clock ticking down and spectators holding their breath, Emma executed a brilliant move that left Alex in a checkmate. The room erupted in applause, not just for the winner but for the indomitable spirit of chess that had bound the town together.

The Checkmate Chronicles of Alex and Emma became a legendary tale in Brooksville, inspiring generations of young minds to explore the world of chess. The community center continued to echo with the click of chess pieces and the laughter of young champions, ensuring that the legacy of Alex and Emma lived on, eternally imprinted on the town's chessboard of memories.

22. Synchronized Dreams: Lily and Mia's Swimming Synchrony

Once upon a time in the charming town of Harborville, two inseparable friends, Lily and Mia, shared a love for the water that went beyond the ordinary. They spent their days swimming in the local pool, where their passion for synchronized swimming began to bloom.

Lily, with her chestnut hair and eyes the color of the deep ocean, was known for her elegant strokes and graceful movements. Mia, with her infectious laughter and auburn curls, complemented Lily perfectly with her lively and expressive routines. Together, they formed an unspoken bond, a connection that extended beyond friendship – it was a synchrony that unfolded seamlessly in the water.

Their journey into synchronized swimming began when they stumbled upon an old book in the dusty corner of the town library. The pages were filled with illustrations of graceful swimmers moving in perfect harmony, creating intricate shapes and patterns beneath the water's surface. Lily's eyes sparkled with excitement as she shared her newfound discovery with Mia.

Determined to bring the beauty of synchronized swimming to life, Lily and Mia approached Coach Harper at the Harborville Aquatic Club. Intrigued by their enthusiasm, Coach Harper agreed to mentor the dynamic duo. Under her guidance, Lily and Mia began practicing tirelessly, mastering the art of synchronization.

Their routine became a mesmerizing display of fluidity and precision. Lily and Mia spent hours perfecting every spin, twirl, and lift, seamlessly blending their movements to create a visual poetry in the water. The poolside would often fill with applause as the townsfolk gathered to witness the magic that unfolded every day at the Harborville Aquatic Club.

As their skills blossomed, Lily and Mia's reputation as synchronized swimmers spread beyond Harborville. Invitations poured in for them to showcase their talent at regional competitions. The duo embraced the opportunity, excited to share their love for synchronized swimming with a broader audience.

Competing on a larger stage brought new challenges. Lily and Mia faced formidable opponents, each with their own unique styles. But the bond between them proved unbreakable. No matter the pressure, Lily and Mia found solace in each other's presence, and their synchrony shone brighter than ever.

The day of the regional competition arrived, and the Harborville Aquatic Club buzzed with anticipation. Lily and Mia took to the water, their bodies moving as one, telling a story of friendship and shared dreams. The audience was captivated, and as the final notes of their routine echoed through the venue, a standing ovation erupted.

Lily and Mia's synchronized dreams had not only enchanted their hometown but had also earned them accolades and recognition in the wider world of synchronized swimming. They became an inspiration for aspiring swimmers everywhere, proving that true synchrony goes beyond movements – it's a shared passion, a harmony of hearts.

As the sun set on their remarkable journey, Lily and Mia continued to swim side by side, their synchronized dreams evolving into a lifelong celebration of friendship, perseverance, and the magic that happens when two hearts beat as one in the water.

23. Golfing Green: Jack, Zoe, and the Greenside Adventure

Once upon a sunny summer day in the quiet town of Fairview, two inseparable friends, Jack and Zoe, found themselves captivated by the lush, green expanse of the local golf course. Little did they know that this serene setting would become the backdrop for an extraordinary adventure that would shape their friendship and ignite a passion for golf like never before.

Jack, a freckle-faced boy with a perpetual grin, had always been fascinated by the precision and skill involved in golf. Zoe, his adventurous counterpart with a perpetual ponytail, was up for any challenge that promised excitement. One day, as they wandered near the golf course, they spotted a friendly old golf pro named Mr. Thompson giving lessons to aspiring young golfers.

Intrigued, Jack and Zoe approached Mr. Thompson, who welcomed them with a warm smile. He sensed their curiosity and offered to teach them the basics of golf. Jack eagerly picked up a golf club, feeling its weight in his hands, while Zoe marveled at the smoothness of the golf balls.

Under Mr. Thompson's patient guidance, the duo discovered the art of a perfect swing, the importance of proper posture, and the thrill of seeing the ball soar through the air. As their skills developed, so did their love for the game. The golf course became their haven, a place where laughter echoed across the greens, and the camaraderie between Jack, Zoe, and Mr. Thompson flourished.

One sunny afternoon, Mr. Thompson surprised the duo with an invitation to a local junior golf tournament. Excitement bubbled within them as they prepared to showcase their newfound talents. The tournament day arrived, and Fairview's golf course buzzed with youthful energy. Jack and Zoe, clad in their matching golf attire, stepped up to the tee with determination in their eyes.

The tournament proved to be a challenging yet exhilarating experience. Each swing, each putt, brought them closer to the dream of victory. Their families and the townsfolk cheered them on, witnessing the growth of two friends who had transformed from curious onlookers to formidable young golfers.

As the final holes approached, Jack and Zoe found themselves tied for the lead. The pressure was intense, but their shared journey and the support of the community fueled their determination. On the 18th hole, with a gallery of spectators watching, they took their shots with unwavering focus.

In a breathtaking moment, Jack's ball rolled into the cup, securing his victory. The crowd erupted into cheers as Jack beamed with pride. Zoe, though narrowly missing the win, celebrated her friend's success with genuine joy. They had not only discovered the thrill of victory but also the beauty of friendly competition and the camaraderie that golf fosters.

The Greenside Adventure became a defining chapter in Jack and Zoe's friendship. They continued to play golf, sharing countless more laughs and victories, all while nurturing their love for the game that had brought them together. The golf course, once a simple backdrop, had become a tapestry of memories—a place where dreams were launched and friendships solidified, proving that sometimes, the most extraordinary adventures unfold in the most unexpected places. And so, in the heart of Fairview, Jack, Zoe, and the Greenside Adventure continued to inspire the young and young-at-heart to swing for the stars and chase the thrill of the perfect golfing green.

24. Equestrian Echoes: Olivia, Jake, and the Horseback Harmony

Once upon a time in the picturesque town of Brooksville, nestled against rolling hills and surrounded by meadows, lived two adventurous youngsters named Olivia and Jake. Their lives were destined to intertwine through a shared love for the enchanting world of horses and the captivating art of equestrianism.

Olivia, with her flowing chestnut hair and sparkling hazel eyes, had grown up on the outskirts of town. From a young age, she felt an undeniable connection to the graceful creatures that roamed the vast, green pastures surrounding her home. Her afternoons were spent watching the horses gallop freely, their manes dancing in the wind.

On the other side of Brooksville, in a cozy farmhouse with a red barn, lived Jake—a spirited and curious boy with a mop of unruly blonde hair and a perpetual twinkle in his blue eyes. Jake's affinity for adventure led him to explore the nearby forests and fields, where he often stumbled upon equestrian competitions and horse shows.

It was during the annual Brooksville County Fair that Olivia and Jake's paths crossed for the first time. The fairgrounds buzzed with excitement as families gathered to celebrate the community's rich agricultural heritage. Among the festivities, the equestrian event stood out with its display of magnificent horses and skilled riders.

Olivia, mesmerized by the sight of the riders gracefully guiding their horses through intricate patterns, dreamt of one day becoming a skilled equestrian herself. Jake, who had ventured to the fair seeking new adventures, found himself captivated by the beauty and power of the horses that seemed to move in perfect harmony with their riders.

A chance encounter near the stables brought Olivia and Jake together. Olivia, who had been observing the horses with a wistful gaze, noticed Jake's keen interest and struck up a conversation. Their shared passion for horses and the dream of mastering the art of riding created an instant bond between them.

Inspired by their newfound friendship, Olivia and Jake began attending equestrian classes together. Under the guidance of a wise and experienced riding instructor named Mr. Thompson, they learned the art of horseback riding, grooming, and forming a deep connection with their equine companions.

As the days turned into weeks, and the weeks into months, Olivia and Jake's skills flourished. They practiced trotting, cantering, and jumping with boundless enthusiasm, their laughter echoing through the stables and meadows. The horses, too, seemed to respond to their riders' joy, forging a unique bond that transcended words.

One sunny afternoon, Mr. Thompson announced an upcoming equestrian competition—the prestigious Brooksville Equestrian Showcase. Excitement filled the air as Olivia and Jake seized the opportunity to showcase their newfound talents. The prospect of participating in the event fueled their determination to succeed.

The days leading up to the showcase were filled with intense practice sessions, bonding moments with their horses, and a shared sense of anticipation. Olivia and Jake encouraged each other through every hurdle, finding solace and inspiration in the supportive harmony they had created within their equestrian journey.

Finally, the day of the Brooksville Equestrian Showcase arrived. The fairgrounds, transformed into an arena of elegance, echoed with the rhythmic beats of hooves and the cheers of the crowd. Olivia, dressed in a regal riding outfit, and Jake, donning a crisp equestrian ensemble, felt a mixture of nervousness and excitement as they entered the competition arena.

As the duo gracefully guided their horses through the intricate patterns, a magical connection unfolded. The audience watched in awe as Olivia and Jake, with synchronized movements, showcased the beautiful harmony they had achieved with their equine companions. It was a performance that transcended competition—it was a celebration of friendship, passion, and the timeless connection between humans and horses.

The judges, deeply moved by the enchanting display, awarded Olivia and Jake with the coveted Harmony Cup—a symbol of their exceptional bond and skillful equestrian artistry. The cheers of the crowd and the proud neighs of their horses echoed through the fairgrounds, marking a triumphant moment in the lives of these young equestrians.

As the sun set over Brooksville, casting a warm glow on the meadows and stables, Olivia and Jake reflected on their journey. The echoes of their equestrian adventure had created not only lasting memories but also a profound understanding of the magic that happens when passion, friendship, and the spirit of adventure converge.

And so, in the heart of Brooksville, where meadows met rolling hills, the echoes of Olivia, Jake, and the horseback harmony lingered—a timeless tale of two kindred spirits and the enchanting world of equestrian dreams.

25. Marathon Mates: Ethan, Ava, and the Long Run to Victory

Once upon a time, in the quaint town of Everwood, two inseparable friends, Ethan and Ava, discovered a shared passion for running that would lead them on an incredible journey of determination, friendship, and triumph.

Ethan, a lanky and energetic boy with a perpetual smile, had always been captivated by the rhythmic beat of his running shoes hitting the pavement. Ava, a spirited girl known for her boundless enthusiasm, found solace and joy in the wind brushing against her face as she sprinted through the local park.

One sunny afternoon, the two friends decided to join the Everwood Kids' Marathon, an annual event that drew young runners from all corners of the town. The marathon was not just a race; it was a celebration of community, perseverance, and the spirit of achieving personal goals.

Excitement bubbled within Ethan and Ava as they registered for the marathon. They were eager to challenge themselves and, more importantly, to experience the joy of crossing the finish line hand in hand.

As the training days unfolded, Ethan and Ava, now known as the "Marathon Mates," embraced the rigors of running. They woke up at dawn, laced up their sneakers, and jogged through Everwood's picturesque streets. The duo set goals, pushed each other to overcome obstacles, and reveled in the small victories of increased endurance and improved speed.

Their journey to the marathon became more than just a physical feat; it became a testament to the strength of their friendship. Through sweat, laughter, and occasional setbacks, Ethan and Ava discovered that the true essence of victory lay not just in reaching the finish line but in the shared moments and support that fueled their run.

The day of the Everwood Kids' Marathon arrived, and the town buzzed with excitement. Families lined the streets, cheering for every young runner who passed by. Among the crowd, Ethan's and Ava's families held handmade signs that read, "Go Marathon Mates!"

As the starting gun echoed through the air, Ethan and Ava embarked on their 26.2-mile adventure. The marathon tested their endurance, but the cheers from the sidelines and the shared determination kept them going. At each mile marker, the Marathon Mates exchanged glances, silently encouraging each other to press on.

In the final stretch, with the finish line in sight, Ethan and Ava locked eyes and, without a word, sprinted hand in hand toward victory. The crowd erupted into cheers as they crossed the finish line, their marathon journey culminating in a triumph that surpassed their wildest dreams.

The Marathon Mates, now Everwood's local heroes, shared a moment of joy, exhaustion, and accomplishment. Their journey had not only strengthened their friendship but had also inspired the entire town to believe in the power of perseverance and camaraderie.

And so, in the heart of Everwood, the legend of Marathon Mates, Ethan and Ava, lived on—a story of two friends who, through the long run of life, discovered that victory was not just about reaching the destination but savoring every step of the journey together.

26. Basket of Dreams: Sarah, James, and the Wheelchair Slam Dunk

In the vibrant town of Crestwood, where the rhythmic sounds of bouncing basketballs echoed through the neighborhood, lived two extraordinary friends, Sarah and James. They shared a bond that extended far beyond the basketball court, a friendship rooted in a shared love for the game and an unyielding spirit that knew no bounds.

Sarah, a spirited and determined young girl, had been using a wheelchair since a young age due to a congenital condition. Despite the challenges she faced, her infectious enthusiasm and unwavering passion for basketball never waned. She had an uncanny ability to see possibilities where others saw limitations, and it was this optimism that drew her to the local basketball court every day.

James, a compassionate and kind-hearted boy, was drawn to Sarah's indomitable spirit. He recognized in her a fierce competitor and a genuine love for the game. Unlike many others, James saw Sarah not for her wheelchair but for the incredible athlete and friend that she was.

The two friends spent countless afternoons on the court, practicing dribbles, perfecting passes, and dreaming of achieving the seemingly impossible — a wheelchair slam dunk. It became their shared dream, a goal that fueled their tireless efforts to break barriers and challenge stereotypes.

As word spread through the community about Sarah and James' aspiration, the town rallied behind them. Local businesses donated a specially designed basketball wheelchair, and the town council renovated the basketball court to make it more accessible. The support was overwhelming, and the duo felt the weight of their community's hopes resting on their shoulders.

Sarah and James faced numerous obstacles as they worked towards their dream. They encountered skeptical onlookers and doubters who couldn't fathom the idea of a wheelchair slam dunk. However, fueled by their unwavering determination, they persevered through every setback, turning negativity into motivation.

The day of the much-anticipated slam dunk attempt arrived, and the entire town gathered at the court, buzzing with excitement. Sarah, with James by her side, rolled onto the court amid cheers and applause. The atmosphere was electric as they took their positions, and the ball was passed between them with seamless precision.

In a breathtaking moment that seemed to defy gravity itself, Sarah launched into the air with the ball in her hands, and, with James providing crucial support, executed a perfect slam dunk. The crowd erupted in cheers, and tears of joy flowed freely. It was a moment of triumph not just for Sarah and James but for the entire community that had come together to witness the power of dreams and perseverance.

The story of Sarah, James, and the wheelchair slam dunk became an inspiration far beyond Crestwood. It spread through social media, capturing the hearts of people around the world. The dynamic duo continued to advocate for inclusivity in sports, proving that with passion, teamwork, and unwavering belief, dreams could indeed be transformed into reality.

"Basket of Dreams" became a symbol of hope, a tale that reminded everyone that limitations are only as powerful as the belief in overcoming them. Sarah and James, through their extraordinary journey, taught the world that the true measure of a slam dunk lies not just in the height reached but in the courage it takes to defy expectations and soar above them.

27. Kite Soaring: Skylar, Leo, and the High-Flying Adventure

In the picturesque coastal town of Cresthaven, where the salty breeze danced with the waves, two inseparable friends, Skylar and Leo, found themselves captivated by the mesmerizing dance of colorful kites in the expansive sky. As the sun dipped below the horizon, casting hues of orange and pink, the duo felt an unspoken connection with the soaring kites that seemed to touch the very fabric of the evening sky.

Skylar, with her unruly curls and infectious laughter, had always been drawn to the freedom that kites symbolized. Leo, her thoughtful and tech-savvy companion, shared her fascination. Together, they dreamed of mastering the art of kite flying and creating a spectacle that would rival the most vibrant sunsets.

Their journey began with a weathered kite shop at the edge of town, where an elderly man named Mr. Fletcher welcomed them with a twinkle in his eye. Mr. Fletcher, a seasoned kite enthusiast, sensed the passion burning in Skylar and Leo's hearts. He bestowed upon them an antique kite, its paper wings whispering tales of adventures from years gone by.

Under Mr. Fletcher's watchful eye, Skylar and Leo embraced the challenge of mastering the intricate dance of wind and string. The duo spent their afternoons on the windswept cliffs, where Skylar's kite gracefully soared, its tail swirling like a comet's tail. Leo, armed with a high-tech GPS, documented every twist and turn, transforming their escapade into a high-flying adventure.

As Skylar and Leo's skills blossomed, so did their friendship. The duo began experimenting with innovative kite designs, incorporating LED lights to illuminate the night sky. Soon, the sleepy town of Cresthaven buzzed with excitement about the dynamic duo and their nightly kite performances.

Their fame reached the ears of the town's annual kite festival organizers, who extended an invitation for Skylar and Leo to showcase their unique creations. Thrilled by the prospect of sharing their passion on a grand scale, the friends poured their hearts into crafting an awe-inspiring spectacle for the festival.

The day of the festival arrived, and Cresthaven's sky transformed into a canvas of color, illuminated by Skylar and Leo's dazzling kites. The crowd marveled at the intricate choreography of the glowing kites, each movement telling a story of friendship, dreams, and the boundless possibilities that soared with every gust of wind.

Skylar and Leo's high-flying adventure had not only brought joy to Cresthaven but had also taught the townsfolk the magic of pursuing one's dreams with unwavering determination. As the festival came to an end, Skylar and Leo realized that their journey had only just begun.

With the lessons learned from their kite-soaring escapades, Skylar and Leo continued to explore the skies, inspiring others to look up and dream. Together, they discovered that the true magic of their high-flying adventure wasn't just in the kites that painted the sky but in the friendship that soared to new heights with every flight.

And so, against the backdrop of the setting sun and the whispering waves, Skylar and Leo's kites continued to dance, reminding everyone that dreams, like kites, have the power to soar beyond the horizon and touch the stars.

28. Martial Arts Marvels: Maya, Ethan, and the Artful Combat

Once upon a time in the vibrant city of Zenithville, two inseparable friends, Maya and Ethan, discovered the ancient and mystical world of martial arts. The sun cast long shadows over the dojo as they stepped inside, drawn by the rhythmic echoes of disciplined movements and the faint scent of incense that permeated the air.

Maya, with her ebony hair tied in a determined bun, and Ethan, his hazel eyes filled with curiosity, were greeted by the wise Sensei Akira. The elderly martial arts master saw potential in the spirited duo and decided to take them under his wing.

Their journey began with the basics – disciplined stances, focused breathing, and the art of emptying one's mind. The dojo became a second home for Maya and Ethan, who embraced the teachings not just as physical exercises but as a way of life.

Sensei Akira introduced them to various martial arts styles — from the swift strikes of Kung Fu to the precise kicks of Taekwondo. Maya's agility shone in the fluid movements of Kung Fu, while Ethan's strength found expression in the powerful kicks of Taekwondo. They were martial arts marvels in the making.

As Maya and Ethan delved deeper into their training, they encountered challenges that extended beyond the physical. They learned about the importance of respect, humility, and the unspoken bond between a martial artist and their art. Each lesson was a step towards not just mastering techniques but also understanding the philosophy that underscored the artful combat they were part of.

One day, the city faced a looming threat as a group of mischievous troublemakers known as the Shadow Serpents emerged. Their leader, the cunning Cobra Kai, aimed to wreak havoc and chaos upon Zenithville. The citizens were in fear, and the city needed its heroes.

Maya and Ethan, having honed their skills under Sensei Akira, felt the weight of responsibility upon their shoulders. They knew it was time to put their training into action and protect the city they loved.

The duo faced the Shadow Serpents in a thrilling showdown. Maya's swift strikes and Ethan's powerful kicks became a dance of artful combat, a symphony of movement that left their adversaries bewildered. The battle was not just physical; it was a test of character, determination, and the values instilled in them by Sensei Akira.

As Maya and Ethan stood victorious, the city erupted in cheers. Zenithville had found its martial arts marvels, and Maya and Ethan realized that being a hero wasn't just about defeating villains but about embodying the principles they had learned in the dojo.

From that day forward, Maya and Ethan continued their journey as martial artists, not just mastering the artful combat but also using their skills to inspire others. Sensei Akira watched with pride as his two pupils became the guardians of Zenithville, the living embodiment of the ancient martial arts wisdom that transcends time.

And so, the legend of Martial Arts Marvels Maya and Ethan continued, their story echoing through the city like the rhythmic beats of a martial arts kata, a testament to the power of discipline, friendship, and the artful combat that resides within us all.

29. Aerial Adventures: Lily, Leo, and the Circus Sky Spectacle

In a small town nestled between rolling hills and a canopy of endless skies, two friends, Lily and Leo, discovered the magic that lived within the art of circus performance. From a young age, Lily had been fascinated by the graceful movements of aerialists, their daring acrobatics soaring through the air. Leo, her equally adventurous friend, shared her passion for the extraordinary.

One sunny afternoon, as the vibrant hues of a setting sun painted the town, Lily stumbled upon an old, dusty circus tent pitched on the outskirts. Drawn by an invisible force, she convinced Leo to join her in exploring this forgotten world of wonder.

Inside the tent, the air buzzed with the enchanting echoes of laughter and music from days gone by. Lily and Leo felt an instant connection to the lively energy that still lingered in the air. As they ventured further, they stumbled upon a weathered, but still magnificent, trapeze.

Their eyes widened with excitement, and without hesitation, Lily and Leo decided to embark on a journey to revive the circus spirit. They tirelessly practiced, swinging from the trapeze, twirling through the air with the grace of aspiring aerialists. As their skills grew, so did their dreams of showcasing their talents to the town.

Word of their aerial prowess spread, and soon, the entire community was buzzing with anticipation. Lily and Leo were determined to put on a circus sky spectacle that would transport their neighbors to a world of magic and wonder.

The big day arrived, and the town gathered under the grand circus tent. The atmosphere was charged with excitement and curiosity. Lily and Leo, adorned in glittering costumes, climbed the trapeze ladder with hearts pounding but spirits soaring.

As they swung through the air, executing breathtaking twists and turns, the audience was transported into a realm of awe. Gasps of delight echoed under the tent, and the vibrant energy of the circus revived in full force. Lily and Leo's aerial adventure had become a spectacle of joy, inspiring everyone to believe in the extraordinary possibilities that lived within each of them.

The circus sky spectacle became an annual tradition, a celebration of bravery, friendship, and the magical spirit that resided in Lily, Leo, and the hearts of their entire community. Lily and Leo had not only brought the circus back to life but had also created a lasting legacy of dreams taking flight in the small town beneath the endless skies.

30. Triathlon Team: Maya, Liam, Zoe, and the Ultimate Race Challenge

In the quaint town of Riverside, nestled between rolling hills and crystal-clear lakes, there lived three friends who shared an unbreakable bond: Maya, Liam, and Zoe. They were known for their adventurous spirits and a love for challenges that pushed their limits. Little did they know, their lives were about to take a thrilling turn as they discovered the world of triathlons.

Maya, a passionate swimmer with a love for water that rivaled the sea itself, spent her weekends gliding through the town's lake with the grace of a mermaid. Liam, a tireless cyclist, explored every hidden trail and winding road, his trusty bike by his side. Zoe, a natural-born runner, sprinted through fields and forests, her heart pounding with each stride.

One sunny afternoon, as the trio lounged by the lake after a day of individual training, a flyer caught Maya's eye. It announced the first annual Riverside Triathlon – a challenging race encompassing swimming, cycling, and running. The excitement among the friends was palpable, and they knew instantly that this was the ultimate challenge they had been waiting for.

With determination ablaze in their eyes, Maya, Liam, and Zoe began their intensive training regimen. The lake became their second home, the trails their playground, and the town's streets their racecourse. Each day brought new challenges, but their friendship and shared goal kept them going.

As the day of the Riverside Triathlon approached, the town buzzed with anticipation. Residents cheered for the hometown heroes who dared to take on the ultimate race challenge. The atmosphere was electric as Maya, Liam, and Zoe stood at the starting line, their hearts pounding in unison.

The sound of the starting horn echoed through the air, marking the beginning of their journey. Maya dove into the lake, her strokes powerful and rhythmic. Liam mounted his bike, his legs pumping with determination as he conquered the hilly terrain. Zoe took off on the run, her feet barely touching the ground as she raced through the streets.

The triathlon was more than a physical challenge; it was a test of their friendship, resilience, and the unwavering belief that together they could conquer anything. As Maya emerged from the water, Liam breezed through the cycling course, and Zoe approached the final stretch of the run, the trio felt a surge of pride and accomplishment.

In a triumphant finish, Maya, Liam, and Zoe crossed the finish line together, arms raised in celebration. The cheers of the crowd mixed with their laughter as they embraced the sweet taste of victory. The Riverside Triathlon wasn't just a race; it was a testament to the strength of friendship, the power of teamwork, and the joy of pushing oneself beyond limits.

As the sun set over Riverside, casting a warm glow on the triumphant trio, Maya, Liam, and Zoe knew that this was just the beginning of their journey. The ultimate race had not only tested their physical abilities but had also solidified a bond that would last a lifetime. Together, they proved that with courage, determination, and the support of true friends, every challenge could be turned into an exhilarating adventure.